Aryla Publishing © 2017

www.arylapublishing.com
Visit the site for more information on
books by <u>Tyler Moses</u> and to be informed
of free promotions!

For all those who dream of success and wealth becoming a gold digger may seem easy but is harder than it seems.

Please see other books by

Tyler Moses

How to Get a Rich Woman
How to be a World Leader (Coming Soon!)

Please see other Titles from
ARYLA PUBLISHING

Childrens Books
The Body Goo Series
The Billy Series

Adult Books
Self Help Books
Diet and Wellbeing

How to Be a Gold Digger

Table of Contents

Chapter 1: What is a Gold Digger?

As Benjamin Franklin famously stated, there are two certainties in life: death and taxes. An uplifting vision that most working-class people spend their lives trying to avoid. Employment is their window to opportunity and they work to live but, as life begins to weigh them down, it ends up being that they live to work. Nobody wants to approach the end of their life having wasted a majority of their time working but, alas, this is a tale as old as the hills. There is, however, one tried and trusted way to ensure that you live your life walking among some of the wealthiest and most successful people without ever having wasted a day cooped up in a cubicle, dealing with the office quack job, or biting your tongue when a boss delves out unrealistic deadlines. Become a gold digger.

Now that might sound like an easy option, but becoming a gold digger is not as simple as putting on your favorite cocktail apparel and watching the wallets magnetize your way. In fact, gold digging demands intricate layers of skill and ability; it isn't just anyone with a pretty face who can pull it off.

Here we will cover everything you need to know in order to be a successful gold digger, but first let's take a detailed look at what a gold digger actually is.

A gold digger is commonly thought of as someone that chooses who to marry based on wealth, but in reality, concerns much more than getting someone to place that ring on your finger. It is a deception that demands high degrees of perception and a versatile range of characteristics, including highly-refined social skills, the ability to adapt to any situation and to understand the needs and anxieties lurking within the outer shell of someone who has achieved wealth and success. A gold digger must become a party chameleon, succeeding in being a memorable part of any event or encounter, while appearing to make such an impact effortlessly. If at any point your wealthy suitor is onto your mating dance then the game will be given away and the dig will unearth nothing except a lot of hard work and disappointment. You must be an archaeologist and actor at the same time, performing flawlessly while certain that your detection skills are sound.

No craft is easily obtained without dedication, but take heart. Like most things in life, status is a construct and no contender starts off in a position of ease and convenience. Today's high-flying celebrity man-eater once had nothing but your typical asymmetrical face, B sized breasts, and dirty blonde hair. Her body might have been young and beautiful, but she didn't stick out in a crowd – with all the 'talent' out there in the world, she had landed smack dab in the middle of average and in gold digger hell. So very far away from that union with the rich lawyer of her dreams – but she did not let that stop her. Those years spent perfecting her craft – practicing her social interactions, working towards the perfect face and body, and learning how to give the illusion of love at first sight – have paid off. She is now a master of her art-form, from that first jaw-dropping meeting, right down to knowing the perfect smells and the ideal food and drink for attracting the best catch.

Since transforming from that dirty blonde that looked like she could be anybody's, Miss Destined to Marry a Billionaire has proven adept at monetizing for the purposes of enhancing her physical appearance and social skills. Perhaps a small amount of money has enabled her to invest in breast augmentation or liposuction, but if not then she has researched exactly how to make the most of her appearance anyway, in order to be the prize in the room that every straight man would want to enter and leave it with. She may have even increased her arsenal by putting some hard work into picking up skills that will support her endeavors, like learning how to cook. Consequently, she is a poor, hot girl no more, but a force to be reckoned with.

Even so, there is still the question of vision and strategy for every wannabe. Only one wife at a time per rich guy, after all – unless you'd prefer to go for the mistress angle. Gold diggers must, therefore, have a clear scale on which to place their ambitions. The richer a gold digger aims, the more competition they will need to overcome.

The greater the beast within your sights, the more substantial the conflict and less certain the return on investment. The more elaborate and choreographed the fellow birds of paradise operating in your neck of the woods, the less likely your own perfect transformation will be the one that attracts your desired mate. Being a gold digger demands finding your own playing field, where you can be confident about being physically, emotionally, and socially ahead of the competition. Failure and misjudgments can prove expensive, rendering any personal and financial investment obsolete – even girls not looking for true love can end up broken hearted.

But there is a silver lining to paying all this time and attention to craft and research, which is that, regardless of how many stories there are of rich boys getting into nasty divorce suits, or even the occasional wise head who suspects you might not quite be what you seem, the likelihood is that no one will see you coming. People too readily assume that the gold digger is a brainless and lazy beast, but you will be smart, focused and so overwhelmingly hot that, when the time is right, your prey will simply fall right into your hands. Because the male ego wants him to be standing next to the hottest ticket in the room, regardless of how smart he is. Remember, for guys, being smart and acting smart are two separate things entirely.

Compare your task to that of a young entrepreneur, who will waste away their days struggling to provide goods and/or services that meet the expectations of hundreds, thousands, maybe even millions of customers. In contrast, the gold digger has one customer and they only need to concern themselves with providing goods and services that meet the needs of that one wealthy person. The rest of their time (and now money) can be spent to their heart's content. A casual trip to the Bahama's? Sure. A new addition to your sports car collection? Not a problem. Season passes to Disney? Absolutely. The gold digger makes memories, while the employed individual wastes them. That's a life of money well spent.

Every bird dances to a different song; some dubstep, and some twerk. It just so happens that a gold digger dances to the sound of money. That doesn't mean that the gold digger cannot be truly in love with their chosen significant other. Money represents power and the power to live an easy life; to access significant goods and/or services, or to have influence over a population. There are numerous common interests between a gold digger and their mate. They both desire power. They may go about obtaining that power through different means but, ultimately, it is power that brings them together and fuels their relationship. Some may find this type of relationship less than desirable. But to the power hungry, it's close to perfect. Besides, no one's ever truly figured out what is the right or wrong way to love... even the great bard remained utterly confused.

Being a gold digger will require a few years of investment, for a lifetime of return. Most people say you can't put a price on true love, well then who wants that? Your love will have a retain value gross and net. So, now that you understand what a gold digger is, and the complex lifestyle that they must keep, we can move on and look into how to become a gold digger.

Chapter 2: How to Become a Gold Digger

Becoming a gold digger is a lifestyle choice that will require some investment into your physical appearance, along with some research into which rich person you plan to make your snuggle bunny. Once you have decided that the gold digger life is for you, then everything else will begin to fall into place accordingly. Maybe you have grown tired of being a part of the low middle/income people. Maybe you have an overwhelming desire to become an influencer of some sort. Maybe you're being hunted by the mafia. Whatever your motivation, choosing to live life as a gold digger is the first step to success… or failure. So, what will your own path look like? There is only one way to find out!

To ensure a wealthy life, treat your gold digging transition like a business venture and less like a love cruise. Such an approach will keep your mind on task and will help you keep your eye on the prize. A love cruise, on the other hand, might harm your focus, whereas it's best to start off with a detailed plan and stick to it.

To establish a plan, first set yourself an end goal, using the criteria of S.M.A.R.T (specific, measurable, attainable, realistic and time constrained).

For example, "The goal is to marry a doctor who owns his own practice and makes over $6 million a year, before I am 25 years old." Notice how I did not leave the profession or income amount open for interpretation. The goal is specific; and rest assured that there will be a man who fits into your category – there always is.

The next step is to establish a means to get there fast and efficiently; gold diggers are hunters not dawdlers. If you are cut out for this, then being completely unsatisfied with your current lifestyle will be motivation enough to ensure that you will have purpose behind your every move. Know exactly what it is that you're working toward, without aiming too high with the income amount either. You can always increase that once you have your first marriage in the bag. "But, what if I fall in love with the first person…?" you might ask. You won't; he only makes $6 million dollars so get with the game. All gold diggers should become familiar with 'the leapfrog effect'.

Now that you have your S.M.A.R.T goal set, it is time to conduct a situation analysis. Consider and write down your current financial and lifestyle situation. The way you look, the friends you have, the car you drive, the house and neighborhood you live in; all of the fine details that revolve around your current day-to-day life. For each of the details you write down, using your S.M.A.R.T goals, decide how you want each of them to look once you have become a successful gold digger. Be brutal; assess your looks, friends, your car and your property, then decide what they should be in five years' time.

Here's an example, let's say you currently live in a house that is worth $55,000 in a neighborhood that has an annual income of <$40,000. You may want to live in a house that is worth $1.5 million within a neighborhood that has an annual income of <$8million once you are a gold digger. If you drive a nine-year-old Ford Focus, maybe you want your gold digger car to be a brand-new Lincoln MKX.

Don't hold back from going for exactly what you want – and don't avoid adding children into the equation. If you want them, use them. They will be your best form of leverage while negotiating neighborhood, house and car size, and then later they will be a great tool in helping you get the most out of your divorce. In the long run, what works best for you will only benefit them, so you can afford to be shameless in this respect. Just make sure that your plans include a nanny being the one who spends time with them while they are going through that awful diaper, crying, vomiting phase.

Once these goals and preferences are set, you can move on to the next crucial stage of your plan: assessing the competition. Now that you have all the fine details established, you can use them to keep you one step ahead of your rivals – and yes, they will be out there. Competition will become more fierce as you get closer to your goals. So, it is important to prepare for this, which is why your next step is to do a competitive analysis. Gather all of the information you can about other gold diggers in your area and do a S.W.O.T. analysis on them. This is meant to expose their Strengths, Weaknesses, Opportunities and Threats. In Chapter 1, I briefly mentioned that, in order to be the best of the best, you will need to shine bright enough to stand out in a crowd and leave a lasting impression. What better way to stand out than by making your competition look like common street trash? Knowing the aesthetic and social strengths of who you are up against is critical in making sure that their efforts leave them as an average contender, while you walk away with the prize.

Do not be intimidated by the competitive aspect, instead consider the strengths of your competitors to be useful in order to acquire a base line for your efforts. Confidence comes from knowing that you are one step ahead of them, so, if your competition is known for low cut shirts, you cut yours a little lower – or boost them a little higher. If she has a tight butt, get yourself on a fitness regime that JLo would approve of. Know the fashions and styles that suit you and plan that killer dress or special haircut for when you need to make an impression, not for when you're out shopping and hanging with friends. Of course, you should always take pride in your appearance, but being too noisy at the wrong times risks allowing your rivals to know what they're up against.

Then there's the question of hidden talent. It will prove of great benefit to acquire a skill or hobby that really puts the competition to bed when the play is on. Let's say one of your competitors has an attractive and sexy skill or hobby. So Sally can play the guitar; no problem if you can sit down at a grand piano and serenade an audience with a perfect rendition of Beethoven's Moonlight Sonata. So she's a bit of a thrill seeker and can ride a motorbike; skydiving might be more impressive. Choose your skills to put them on the back foot and don't allow pride to take you somewhere desperate, like convincing yourself you're a good singer when you sound like a strangled cat.

Figuring out an opponent's physical or social falls isn't difficult so long as you have them in your sight. Make sure you are informed enough to go for the jugular. Remember, the early bird gets the worm, but the second mouse gets the cheese. Allow your opponents' weaknesses to bring them down so that you can stomp them out before they become a problem. And if you think "stomping out" the competition is harsh, consider whether they would do the same to you given the chance. There are good and bad choices in the game of gold digging, but no rulebook or referee about to step in and blow his whistle. The saying 'All's fair in love and war,' definitely applies.

Now that you have the information you need on your competitors' strengths and weaknesses, this means that you will also want to do a thorough

S.W.A.T. analysis on yourself. You need to see yourself as others see you and work on improving your weaknesses, minimizing your threats, and making your strengths shine so that you can open up and make the most of many opportunities. This, in essence, is your job interview – a job interview that will ensure you never need an actual job again.

Once you have a thorough S.W.A.T. analysis on yourself and your competition, you should be able to position yourself above anyone that may get in your way of reaching your gold digging goals. You are, truly, going to S.W.A.T. your competition away by developing a list of action items that you will need to execute in order to measure up to the rest. Get a classy yet sexy haircut and color, get your hands and feet smooth and polished, and update your wardrobe. You should also start volunteering your time somewhere within the community. Perception is reality. You must make everyone believe that you are a healthy, fun, and caring individual even if, in reality, you're a monster.

Most likely you will need to put working out and dieting at the top of your list. In order to get more than six figures in salary from your mate, a matching six pack will not go amiss. Being out of shape and showing cellulite, or a tummy, will be detrimental to your cause. But be careful. You don't want to lose too much too fast. You'll have a difficult time explaining extreme weight loss and the sudden two inch thigh gap if rumors start floating around that you're surviving on one leaf of lettuce a day. As in everything, people's perception of you is key. Let your neighbors see you eating an occasional donut or drinking your favorite iced latte. Get a bag of chips from the gas station. Order an extra large pizza from Dominos and eat it all outside while sitting in a lawn chair. Give the perception that you were suddenly blessed with a thyroid disorder or blessed with a month-long illness like pneumonia.

If you understand your gold digger transition as a business venture, it will be easier to find the best path toward a quick marriage with the money of your dreams.

Next, we will discuss what you will need in order to reach your maximum potential, and bring home Richy McDreamy – and don't worry, he'll certainly seem dreamy due to the size of his bank account.

Chapter 3: What you need (props)

Throughout your gold digging journey, it will be critical for you to acquire a few very important props to help you reach your goals. Some of these items are expensive and may require an initial investment. Just remember, if you execute your transition flawlessly, then your return on investment will be well over 100%, so all of your efforts will be worth it.

First and foremost, you need to get rid of your current friends and replace them with better friends. Come on, be honest. Friends can drag you down and make you look bad; it isn't your job to drag them through your own existence if they do nothing for you. Once rid of them, make sure that you replace them with friends of a specific criteria; ones that are well known and trusted in the community, who are ideal for their networking possibilities and who have absolutely no clue about 'the old you' – which is why you should really consider dropping your good friends as well as the bad. Be honest, they tend to come as a group and if they can put you at risk they are not worth the sentiment. The life of a gold digger with a conflict of interest is a ticking time-bomb of failure. There should be no room for them in your life from now on – or in your huge new house.

Ideal new friends include anyone who is very well known, is trusted among their very large circle of friends, and is actively involved in the community. Maybe they serve as president of the local homeless shelter, or volunteer at the local boys and girls club on weekends. You must become their closest friend or this will not work. An honest and caring individual will make you look caring by association – allowing you to be completely the opposite. When the wealthy prospect whose fortune you have eyes on makes enquiries about you, ironically, he will get the false answer from the honest individual – which is exactly the answer you want him to hear.

Second, if you have a social media account, delete it and start a new one. You are changing your life around completely and your social media account is the best way to make people believe that you are who you say you are because, as you know, everything on the internet is true. Your current account is most likely filled with dramatic interactions with your old circle of friends and you can't afford any dirty laundry being unearthed. Just as getting rid of friends gives you a clean slate, so too does new social media, shedding any nasty drama that might otherwise follow you around. Don't get slack or presumptuous on this one. Without fail, you will be looked at on social media by either your rich man in waiting or their family and you only need one seed of doubt to undo all of your hard work. Creating a new profile is the best way for you to get people to believe that you are a good, caring, and fun loving person – because being a good person is too much work. Become a chameleon and change into the perfect person for your goal mate. Social media should not give away too much about you but, what it does, should serve as an advertisement for your catch. So, if they enjoy boating, go boating and post pictures that make it look like it's one of your passions too. If they like to hike, research some great gear and go hike a mountain, documenting the journey. Turn yourself into the perfect woman for him online as well as in the flesh, but avoid too many selfies as that can make you look vain. Or anything too comic which can work against you; better to come across as enigmatic than whacky. Besides, laughing at jokes that aren't funny will be your job.

The third move is: get a gym membership.

And the fourth move is: actually use the gym membership. Your tight curves and tiny tummy aren't going to happen overnight. You will most likely need to lift some weights (light weights to tone your body, not heavy weights that make you look like a lumberjack). It won't hurt to get a personal trainer as well. They can help you work on the areas that you need to improve upon and may offer some dieting advice that will get you on the fast track to pretty and skinny. It also wouldn't be a bad idea to join a spin class or a yoga class. Flexibility never hurt anyone. Keeping yourself involved in different activities is important in building your new image. However, if you have a lot of work to do on your body, make sure you don't get a gym membership at the same gym that your rich mate frequents. Giving away your secrets is never a good idea and, once you have done enough crunches to melt away your muffin top, then you can consider changing gyms to his and making a great impression. Putting yourself through what has become an easy workout, while positioned next to someone who's dripping buckets and desperate to lose the pounds wearing Lycra two sizes too small – never a pretty sight – is a great frame in which to get noticed. Why let such an opportunity pass you by? With one gym to get hot and then another to look hot in, you're well set up to "accidentally" bump into them at an event then can say, "Hey! Don't you go to the gym on 4th street?" When the time comes, such hard work will make the final pieces of the puzzle feel like a breeze.

Next, update your wardrobe. Stop wearing the jeans and sweat shirt that you rocked in high school. Again, be brutal and assume that you've always looked terrible. It's a healthy place to start from because soon you'll feel like a new person as well as looking like one. Keep up with the latest trends in fashion; research what style your goal mate is attracted to and fill your wardrobe with everything from casual attire to what you will need for a black tie affair. You may need to acquire 1 or 2 expensive accessories in order to make this effort successful. You don't want to cheat in that department as your competition will be onto you if you are walking around with a knock-off purse or fake diamond earrings. Cutting corners will give them the opportunity to use that against you. It may benefit you to come up with an interesting story about an accessory. "These pearls used to be my grandmother's. She wore them when she married my grandfather and gave them to me right before they both passed away" or, "My Dad wore this watch during the war. This was the watch they used to time when to storm the beach at Normandy." Storytelling is a great way to create a simple but impactful emotional appeal that people will easily be able to relate to, so make sure you have a repertoire to draw on at the right moment. This will also help you to come across as articulate – your rich guy might be able to get away with mumbled half stories and awkward pauses when he can't find the right words, but your memory banks will be equipped with a lilting eloquence that will soon charm his wallet open.

Lastly, going back to what I mentioned in Chapter 2, you need to acquire a skill. Choose your skill based on the skills of your competition and what is attractive to your prospective rich mate. If you need to learn how to paint, then start taking paint classes. If you need to learn to sing, then take some voice lessons. If you need to learn how to become a taxidermist, then stuff those dead animals all night long! If you keep yourself busy with volunteering, working out, and now with a unique hobby or skill, you may just become the most interesting person in the room. A skill will give you a unique ability that will add to how attractive you become. Don't forget, it's about looking good at a skill, not being good at a skill; the two are totally different things

Your transformation will require a lot of sacrifice, but the rewards are wholly worth it. Think of your old life as the warmup to the proper one you are now destined for and, to kit you up fully, let's move on to talk more about what you should include in your wardrobe.

Chapter 4: How to dress?

As mentioned before, your wardrobe will be the quintessential piece of gold digging power that you will need in order to reach success. Some people like to say, "Don't judge a book by its cover." A good saying perhaps, but there is one saying that's even better, "Please judge a book by its cover. Everybody else does." Sight, unless meeting someone that hasn't showered in a month, is one of the first senses engaged when we meet an individual. It is only natural for us to start trying to figure someone out by what they wear.

Wearing a smock? Clearly an artist. Wearing jazz shoes? Clearly a dancer. Wearing white face paint and a red nose? Clearly a clown... or a serial killer. That is why, at every moment of every day, you must portray the person that you want people to see you as. Your wardrobe is the first line of defense in this effort. The most important thing to keep in mind is that you don't want people to see a gold digger. You want them to see an honest and interesting individual, which is entirely possible so long as you keep any evil laughs in your head.

You need to rid your life of any old, ratty underwear. It may be okay to have some holes in your gold digging game, but those kind of holes are way unacceptable. If you want to look good, then you need to feel good. Be honest, you've been slack on this kind of thing in the past; everyone keeps their socks and underwear too long because it's impossible to plan ahead and know precisely when they will need replacing. Spare at no expense in this department! Your underwear is the first thing you put on and the last thing you take off each day. Feeling good starts with having a sexy and well fitting pair of underwear. If you are getting a gym membership, you are going to be changing in a locker room where other people will see you in your unmentionables. Do not, under any circumstances, allow yourself to be caught in anything close to what some may refer to as, "granny panties", or "whitey tighties". Keep your supply of underwear cute and looking pristine; no Christmas-themed underwear in July or plumping for a different colored bra because you assume no one's going to see. Presumption is a bad habit to get into because no one can really ever predict the circumstances that will reveal the secrets of our undergarments. Additionally, on that score, avoid going too far and wearing anything scandalous. Thongs might look sexy in the right circumstances but you're trying a bit too hard if you're wearing them at the gym, or working the treadmill with some lacy number rather than a proper sports bra – you'll want to protect those babies!

What's important, is that you have a full understanding of what your prospective mate likes to see. If they are the type of person that likes your backside and bosom amplified by what you wear, then make sure you have a good push up bra, some tight shirts, and a few good pairs of tight skinny jeans that can all be paired with some monster high heels. Your work out apparel should also fulfill this prerequisite. While running a 5k in high heels may be the worst decision in human history, some tight "spanks" with a bra that makes the girls sing as you jog on the treadmill will add a nice bang to your arsenal of beautifully bodacious clothing.

Alternatively, maybe you have decided that you are going after a politician, which will demand a wardrobe full of power suits that both your man and the media can respect. Be sure that nothing in your wardrobe will cause your mate any issues in the press. Everything must be tasteful and covering all desirable parts. Your coats can be a tad bit snug and your neck line just above the cleavage; there are ways to look sexy and powerful at the same time. As a politician's other half, it will be very important that you acquire an outfit for all type of occasions that you may need to attend – as well as not being caught wearing the same outfit twice. You might need to go golfing or to a baseball game, which means that you need to get yourself some golf apparel or a baseball cap with some jeans and a nice t-shirt. But consider all angles and avoid any team-related gear, as you don't want to rub anyone up the wrong way. Your catch will not thank you for distracting headlines, even on those occasions when the press are being completely out of line.

And now for your favorite part: shoes. Does it even need to be said? Never underestimate the power of a nice collection of shoes. If you are going to be running outside, keep a few pairs of nice brand name shoes at the ready. More than one pair is needed if your mate likes running on dirt trails. You cannot afford to have dirty or worn-looking shoes, as a surprisingly high percentage of the population do genuinely judge individuals by what's on their feet. When newness has worn off, shows will need to be replaced: no exceptions. You should keep 1 or 2 pairs of brand name running shoes for events that are sneaker appropriate, like at sporting events or for volunteering at a food drive. You will also need to have a few pairs of clean and nice casual shoes that match the outfits that you have to wear at the grocery store.

As a female, the shoes you wear to an upscale event will be one of the most important parts of the outfit you choose. They will tell everyone very intimate details about your likes, dislikes, skills and capabilities. The higher the heel, the crazier you are in bed; the shinier the dress shoe, the more you take care of your personal grooming. Wearing the appropriate shoe is critical for every occasion, so have yourself a collection that will allow you to choose wisely.

However, if there is one aspect of your appearance that is even more important than your shoes then it is certainly your face. Without exception, you will need to wear a flawless face all the time. At the gym, walking your dog, making balloon animals for children in need; whatever you may be doing, you need to always have a face that people adore. This also means that you need to go to great lengths to minimize any blemishes and get all flaws fixed. If you have a big bridge for a nose, get that thing chiseled off right away. Do you have tiny fish lips? Botox those babies until your lips are worthy of being on a Victoria's Secret model. Keep your eyebrows and upper lip waxed and wear colored contacts if your eyes resemble mud.

It's a little weird to wear a full face of makeup to the gym. In order to have a pretty face without the aid of foundation, you need to keep it acne free so that you can get by with the bare minimum of just some mascara and maybe a shiny lip gloss. If you have a history of acne, go see a dermatologist. Remember, there are secrets and techniques for every face-issue you might contend with, so check out all the Internet tips you can find and never stop assessing whether there is room for improvement.

Perfume is an area that can trip some women up. Deodorant is a necessity, but layering other smells on top of it can get overwhelming. Think of it like a scratch and sniff sticker. Strawberry alone smells great and chocolate alone smells delicious. However, you put any of those scents together and they immediately smell like poop covered in glue. Guaranteed. You don't want to be that person who leaves a trail of perfume stink everywhere they go. Your sweet and tempting smell needs to be subtle yet powerful, leaving a lasting and desirable impression. Which is why you need to choose your perfume carefully, and apply it with strategic caution. If you are wearing a scented body lotion, you may be able to get away with a very small dab of perfume behind your ears and on your wrists. Much more than that and you'll have the room sneezing and wafting your chemical trail away. Research for this area is ideal, as perfumes complement your natural chemicals and so different choices suit different people. Be confident enough to go against friendly recommendations if you're sure the stuff doesn't work for you.

Accessorizing also demands considerable thought and attention appropriately. Don't overdo it to the point where you look materialistic. A few items strategically placed will do the trick. A ring or two, some earrings, and a bracelet or watch will be nice for casual affairs. No toe rings though; this is a dangerous area in which to experiment, as those who do usually end up looking like rebellious daughters. So, when you need to be wearing your Sunday best, a necklace with matching earrings that complement your neck line will add the perfect level of class. Subtlety is key.

Lastly, your hair needs to match every occasion and always appear like it's easy to maintain and looks good with little to no effort. This can sometimes be difficult to achieve but, with a few trips to the salon and some tips and tricks from well known stylists, you no longer need to be intimidated by your hair. Be sure to choose a color that will make you stand out without looking like you're the neighborhood birthday party clown. You may need to tame the tiger and get your hair relaxed. Or it's possible that your natural hair is super thin and unpredictable, so maybe some extensions will need to be sewn into your head. For very upscale and fancy events, it's probably wise to go to a stylist to make sure your hair is perfect and will last as long as you need it to. Your stylist, beautician, dermatologist and personal trainer should be on your speed-dial, above next of kin or the state police.

Chapter 5: Where to Find Rich People

The breed of rich person you choose to pursue will determine where you need to go hunting. Let's go over five of the common types of rich people and where you can expect to find them.

We will start with politicians and, as with any type of rich person you go for, it is always crucial not to assume a great fortune. You will need to be certain of wealth, as it's surprising how many public figures, like politicians, actors and celebrities, are not incredibly rich – or even worse, up to their necks in debt.

So, if a politician is self-made, then beware! They may not be as wealthy as they appear to be. This means they are deceiving and, while this suits most politicians, this is not the type of person you want. You don't have enough time for their hard work, perseverance and determination. You will want to go after money-made politicians. Be cunning and check out the ones that partake in political lobbying and large money ventures. You know, the two-faced ones that are probably in good with oil companies and big banks. Everyone screwing each other in a big circle and you can get in on the act, while coming out much cleaner that those who make out they stand 'for the people'.

In order to know where they hang out, you will need to know where the representatives from those big businesses will be. They won't be wasting their time in the community helping better their constituents; that's ridiculous. Most likely, you can find them at large conference centers where a lot of bribing and blackmailing takes place. You can also find them at large events that are usually associated with a national holiday. You'll have to do a little research in order to figure out which is the rich and dirty one fit for his comeuppance. The likelihood is that you'll even come out of it with a squeaky clean public image, as almost all politicians trip up and end up disgraced for one reason or another. When this happens, it's your ticket to that 'leapfrog effect' we talked about. You take the money in a brutal divorce that his public image ensures he falls on the wrong side of, then getting out while keeping the image you have worked so hard to create, except now it is enhanced and for all the world to see. In the wake of his failure he'll see what real power is every time he comes across another newspaper article of you effortlessly winning the public's affection. Then you'll be able to show him you were always far more talented than he ever was at courting publicity and filibustering by putting on your sad face and publicly announcing your ignorance to his dirty deeds.

That's all for the future, of course. For now, just know that politicians are people just like you and I and their choice of lifestyle will completely give away what they are deep down under all the pretense. If you find out that they have a favorite upscale sports bar that is serviced by big-breasted women, then you'll know that it's Wonderbra time when the two of you meet. Maybe they have an expensive taste in food. In that case, you may be able to figure out their favorite store and what days they try to fit in their grocery shopping. Or, if they take pride in physical fitness, then you already know what to do at the gym.

Despite the many options with politicians, their sliminess might turn some of you off. For many, playing the gold digging game with a slick, hot shot lawyer is the greater draw. So let's talk about where you can find them. Lawyers are wealthy and busy people. Which means that pursuing their breed will leave you with a lot of free time to spend their money. Being so busy will require them to have a detailed schedule. If there is one thing that is tried and true about lawyers, it's that they love lunch-time. Most lawyers will have a favorite lunch spot that they escape to every day at the same time. This is where you can easily begin to cross their path. You may also find it beneficial to find out where they park for the day and start bumping into them (not their car) every once in a while. Maybe you luck out and run into car trouble. Your lawyer would love nothing more than to come to the rescue of a damsel in distress, especially if that damsel has followed the gold digger fashion tips. Only remember, you must be on top of your game with a lawyer because – if they're any good – they're skilled at seeing through deception. You don't want to put in all that effort only to find that they've wrapped you around their little finger with the pre-nup, or cunningly tied up their wealth where the divorce lawyers can't find it. Bringing down a lawyer demands that they consider your affections to be true love, but don't worry, their egos are so big that they'll still end up going against their best advice – and turning to a hated rival who you know to be just as good will prove a superb tactic when you want his law to be on your side.

Then there are stock brokers, who might be among some of the wealthiest people and have the potential to be the most sought after in the gold digging world. They are an easy target as they are eager to get a mate that will represent their level of success – you should be licking your lips at the very thought of running into one of these beasts. You want to be careful though as their wealth is subject to market trends. If you choose the wrong one, it's possible that they make a wrong move and lose everything. The most successful stock brokers will be found working somewhere on Wall Street. If you can find a favorite watering hole close to that area then you can take your pick of wealthy mates as they graze and gather for social grooming. Outside of New York City, it will be difficult to find a very successful stock broker, so this target depends upon a well-placed locality for your endeavors.

Doctors are probably the most respected among wealthy people. They may also be some of the hardest to catch though, as they're like Pokemon. If they run their own practice then they have very little time for relationships and are apt to turn away from any strong advances. Knowing where to find doctors can also be tricky, but here is a tip: try a doctor's office. If you are brave enough to cross paths with a doctor as their patient then you can certainly try that method. You will want to be careful though, as many doctors stick to a strict "no dating patients" policy. Doctors tend to get turned off from people they've body-searched for lumps and had to turn to the side and cough, so you will need a good ploy if adopting this route – as much as looking up into his eyes as he presses his stethoscope onto your chest feels like an obvious way to make a connection. Instead, it's best if you find out what their outside interests are and try to work in an encounter that way. Find out if they have a gym that they frequently go to (as you see, this is such a common trend). Doctors also tend to love going to charity events and retreats. If you can catch wind of such information then you can definitely use it to your advantage. Retreats will attract many doctors with an array of backgrounds and interests, opening the doors to many wealthy opportunities.

But lastly, let's talk about the most desired group that every gold digger wishes to mount on their wall: entertainers. Yes, if that sounds like the most fun than that is probably because it is, while there are also a wide range of individuals to choose from. Entertainers is a label that covers an array of professions. Including, but not limited to, athletes, musicians, and actors and/or actresses. In order to find one of these you will need to be a high roller, frequent the expensive clubs, and land an invitation to parties and special awards ceremonies. You will also need to invest quite a bit into yourself if these are the type of fish you aim to catch. After all, most of them are employed to be pretty eye-catching themselves.

Athletes can be found in an array of places. Unfortunately, you will not be able to spark any kind of interest in their place of competition and will need to figure out where they go during their down time in order to gain any traction. During the off season, they probably have a hometown gym that they use to keep themselves in shape and that could be a good place to start. It's possible that they have a favorite club or bar. You will most likely find them with an entourage in one of these places, which makes dealing in these situations tricky, demanding careful strategy – or else a dozen super-hot friends who are all, of course, a tiny bit uglier than you. A tough one to judge when you need to be the most confident person in the room; if you're star struck then this is certainly something you will need to get over in order to function to peak performance. Remember, the only star in your life should be you.

Musicians are a tricky breed of rich also, because they are all so flaky and unpredictable. There are a lot of musicians that carry themselves and spend money as though they have millions of dollars at their disposal, when the reality of their situation is that they live among the millions of want-to-be guitarists and drummers who struggle to keep their finances afloat. Your musician needs to be backed by big names, but headlining their own tour, and have multiple houses scattered throughout two or three countries. You will also have a hard time hunting them down once you start trying to make a move, because they are on tour or frequenting some exotic location most of the time. Of course there are some dates, like award ceremonies, where they can be pinned down at the after parties. Also, don't overlook the managers or producers, as usually they are making far more than the star personas they are hiding behind.

Apart from royalty, actors and/or actresses will be the cream of the crop in the game of gold digging. They are the hardest to achieve, but they come with the best pay off. They are like those rare health drinks you find that actually taste good. You may want to save this catch for after your first divorce. It helps to get your name out there and become somewhat known before you dive in and start fishing in these waters. Actors do like courting other famous people, both seriously and loosely, because sleeping with members of the public so often leads to them hearing about their performance in the media soon afterward.

However, like with musicians, it's hard to know where you can plan to cross paths with an actor and/or actress. Their schedules depend on roles that they have and when or where filming is taking place. One thing that you can always count on though, is that they have an image that is critical to their success. They invest a lot of time and money on keeping themselves in tip top shape so, yet again, the gym is a great option. Remember, they are incredibly vain and love compliments, but coming across as sincere is a must. After all, if they are any good at their craft then they know what a performance is.

The type of rich person that you plan to go after will determine the most likely spots that you can find them. As stated several times, a gym is going to be your best bet for all types of gold digging royalty. However, it's also a safe assumption that they probably do their grocery shopping at an upscale store so it wouldn't be a bad idea to start shopping at one. Now that you know where you can expect to find rich people, let's talk about how to attract these money makers.

Chapter 6: How to Attract Rich People

We have covered in detail the ways that you can use your wardrobe as a form of appeal. It's important that you get the wardrobe right because it will be the first thing that your rich target uses to understand and remember you. This is only the first step, however. Once you have the look that you need, next you need to know how to use it to your advantage. In other words, you've got the tools but do you have the talent?

Dressing in clothes that your rich fishy likes will get you to dip your toe into their pool. It's important to start this process slow, as you don't want to make your actions look or feel intentional. Being honest is what sad, lonely people do. He or she (and more importantly, any family that they have) needs to believe that it was fate that brought you together. The best way to start doing this is to strategically place yourself in one area that your target visits or passes through frequently – though nothing too obvious like their bedroom.

At the onset, subtlety is key. Do not make contact the first few times you try this. Remember, you want them to think that you switched grocery stores for the greater selection of Pop Tarts, not because of them. If they find out you're hunting them down, your efforts will be brought to a screeching halt, unless they happen to be a masochist. At this time, dress in an outfit that is casual, yet powerful, with perfect hair and makeup, and light but memorable scent... but hold back and be patient. Don't make contact the first time they set eyes on you. If so they won't have to be Sherlock Holmes to understand what you might be up to. Instead, it might not so hurt so much even to appear aloof a little, with some dark sunglasses and an absentmindedness that suggests you're not paying much attention to anything.

You want to land yourself in the same aisle or area as them no more than twice. Unofficial scientific studies show that the perfect number is one and a half. This means one meeting in the aisle, plus one casual aisle drive by. It's important to pretend that you don't realize they are there and lead them to believe that you are occupied with something else. Maybe you are reading the ingredients on a can of food or putting sugar in your coffee when you happen to be just a little bit in their way. Then, as they pass by, move slightly out of their path, just enough for them to have the room they need. They have seen you and you haven't caused a distraction. Stage one is complete.

You want to repeat this process once or twice more, but infrequently and certainly not more than once a week. This keeps your interactions subtle and nonchalant until you're ready to take more obvious action. Slow and steady wins the race, or in this case, the money.

All of these efforts are leading up that big move, when you really get into his head. Usually, once you're in there, there will be no turning back for him and most of the hard work will be done. Pressure is now on because this is not just a time to take pride in your craft, but to perform to perfection. The big move is a very delicate process and you'll only get one shot, so you have to make sure your execution is on point. This transaction needs to be smooth and sexy as your interaction is taken into a new environment for the first time. Somewhere they like to go for lunch or dinner perhaps. You might find a lot of success if you attend a benefit, retreat, or gala that your rich person plans to be at. The truth is that these events are actually quite boring, so that should mean that making an impression is that much easier.

You can make your move in one of two ways. The first of which is to do something 'coincidental' so as get their attention, like dropping a book or getting a flat tire. Alternatively, if you choose a club or restaurant to hunt your prey, then your move can be as easy as going up next to them to order food or a drink.

If successful with your stage one transformation, then stage two will fall perfectly into place, like the final pieces of a jigsaw, depicted upon which is your sexy, rich prince. He is a catch who now has a comfortable way of approaching YOU and so the hunted is now becoming the hunter – or so it must look that way for appearances' sake. Once they start to converse with you, all of the research that you carried out when preparing to become a gold digger can at last be drawn upon. Remember your end goal: know your competition and understand completely what the person standing in front of you wants to see and hear. Say all of the right things, make eye contact, laugh at the right time, smile, add in a very light touch on the arm and 'accidentally' compliment his ego in that uncanny way that true love does in the movies. He'll think you're strangely perfect for him, while you'll know there's nothing strange about it at all.

You should have practiced this conversation and know that one word answers are the kiss of death. You should be commenting, not asking, resulting in the kind of dynamic and versatile banter that will draw the exchanges out, rather than ending with yes or no confirmations. Follow up questions with another question, ensuring that awkward silences do not even earn a minor score in the performance. Light teasing is another great addition. For example, "Didn't I see you at the gym? Are you following me?" Continue to give them the opportunity to hit on you and be confident that, because of your hard work, they are seeing something that appears to have everything they are attracted to. Soon, by appearing to show a casual interest, you'll give them the opportunity to talk about themselves and ask you questions so that they can find out that you have similar interests and are a match made in heaven.

So stage 1 saw you dangle the hook in front of their hungry mouths with your rod of beauty and, now, stage 2 is about reeling them in with your charm and personality. Be confident enough to allow them to take their time, even making them work a little, as being patience hides your gold digger intentions. Up until you sign the marriage papers, you need to portray a loving and honest relationship. All of your efforts will be futile if your new spouse suggests a prenuptial agreement. If a prenup is brought into the relationship, you might as well marry your high-school sweetheart who's up to his neck in debt because that band never worked out and he didn't become a rock star like he thought he would. A prenup means you get nothing – especially if you've gone down the route of scoring a hot-shot lawyer. You must take your time to develop a relationship that appears to be filled with love, so that a prenup is the furthest thing from your rich husband's mind as you sign the marriage license.

Chapter 7: How to Get What You Need

We've covered a number of substantial changes that you will need to make in order to become a gold digger and marry a rich person. While some of the changes won't be a financial burden, many of them will require a bit of money. If you're working toward becoming a gold digger, then you probably don't have money which makes many of the necessary changes near impossible. Do not fret though, gold digger in training, there are A LOT of things that you can do to get financial support when becoming a gold digger. So this section will focus on how to make the most of your resources, while exploring what the pitfalls are.

Undoubtedly, a credit card is the easiest and fastest way to get some money. While this won't be enough to fix your witch nose, wizard tits and Hobbit feet, it will help you to get your first few Botox injections, acquire a gym membership, and replace your wardrobe. Now, if you time everything right, you can get 2 or 3 credit cards before they begin to affect your credit and you can no longer apply for new ones. Don't worry about paying it off. When you marry your rich person, they will alleviate you of any existing debt. Also, although the most frugal souls will always advise you to avoid such a reckless approach to life, carrying a bit of risk through your daily outlook does help to incentivize. Which could be important if all your hard work accidentally brings up someone with annoying personal habits or erectile dysfunction. It would be a shame if such unfortunate discoveries made you go right back to the beginning, and having a ticking time-bomb of a credit card will work well to make some of those less enviable discoveries bearable.

Another great route to easy cash flow is inheritance. This will happen to most of us at some point in our lives so, if you're really lucky, then someone will pass away and leave you a portion of their wealth. This then becomes an investment into your future which, when put that way, can't fail to make Grandma happy. Soon your gold digger transformation will be complete. There might be a few awkward comments and observations from the rest of your family when they see you emerging from a period of mourning with a chiseled nose and an increased bust size, but who's going to take charge of your own future if not you?

But of course, it isn't the case that everyone will get this lucky. What can you do if you have bad credit and all of your family is in good health? How do you get the money that you need to support your transformation? Simple answer: ask for it! There are a number of places that will give loans out to people with bad credit. Who cares about the interest rates when in five years you'll be on your third husband? You can even ask a few members of your family for some help. Just tell them that you are investing in you and your unborn child's future, and there will be someone willing to donate a chunk of money to your cause. Asking family is especially successful after the fourth bottle of wine at Christmas, especially if you use the angle that you need that liposuction because your current figure is making you depressed. All of a sudden, an unnecessary procedure to change your body in a way it doesn't need has become a necessary and compassionate move to protect your precious mental well-being.

It might surprise you to learn that this pity approach can also work online. It is amazing what people will donate to via the internet and social media is a great tool to raise funds. "Gofundme" has recently risen as a versatile means of seeking financial support. If you are able to start a gofundme and lead people to believe you are on a mission to locate your own self-esteem, then you have the potential to raise a ton of money to help you with your transformation. If you choose this route, be sure to disguise the creator of the "gofundme" page. Under no circumstances do you want it to point back at you. Even if you have carefully worded the funding campaign to be ethical – under very liberal terminology of course.

Despite this advice, chances are that kickstarting your gold digging will not be so complicated. Maybe you have a cute button nose, your boobs are the perfect size, and a gym membership is all you need to tuck in your tummy and keep your curves curving right. If you're fortunate enough to be born with everything that cultivates primitive attraction, then your only substantial investment needs to be in revamping your wardrobe. If that's your biggest hurdle throughout this process, then you should have no worries and may even be able to aim for very rich people, rather than just the moderately rich to begin with.

Some may suggest picking up your new style at a second hand store to keep the cost down. This is a terrible idea. The clothes that you get at a secondhand store are stretched, faded, and out of date and smell like someone who works at a Little Caesars. They come with frayed edges and armpit stains. The seams of the shirts poke out just enough to make it look like you pulled it off of a 300 pound ox. Any seasoned gold digger will be able to tell when a new cat walks in with pre-owned fur. Buck up and buy new!

Don't buy your wardrobe at a large Walmart Super Center. That's gold digging suicide. Choose well known clothing departments like Bloomingdales, or Macy's for your clothing needs. Their clothing leans toward being high end and classy, while you're also far less likely to have a nightmare clash when turning up at an event – every woman's worst nightmare. You'll be able to dress to impress if you choose clothing stores that will provide you with great brands and styles to fit the image of any rich person's dreams.

If you really mean business, the best way to start over is to get rid of everything that you own. Don't get sentimental; sell and replace. You can sell anything online and, with this kind of lifestyle, re-wearing often is not going to be an option in the long-term anyway. The fashion mags are too vain not to notice such a slip up.

You don't even have to stop at selling clothes: furniture, jewelry, human organs… anything. People love buying any old tat if it's dressed up in the right way. So that old lamp might have been owned by Brittany Spears during her third marriage. Or Princess Di once had a cup of tea when sitting at this table; with a bit of story behind your item someone will cherish it. And this is nothing unusual; it has been estimated that something like 90 percent of memorabilia on eBay is fake, so you're only tapping into a thriving worldwide industry for the convenience of launching a much greater escapade that your average fraudster can only dream about. Getting rid of your stuff will make it really easy to move in with your rich person a few weeks after going home with them for the first time. So this is actually a practical part of the process, unless you're planning on taking all of those turn-up pants into the mansion with you – it would be some turn of events if even the butler feels he can look down his nose at you.

Don't hold back. You can get really creative in the ways that you decide to get what you need in order to become a successful gold digger and, the less you concern yourself with being honest in your efforts, the greater your chance of success. Put all worries about how you're affecting others aside. They don't matter. They are stepping stones to the life you've always wanted – as you would be to most of them if they got the chance. This is about you and your future. As a gold digger, you don't have time to worry about anything other than what rich people want and how you can become one of their most prized possessions. If you lose the respect of loved ones throughout the process, it's not a big deal. You can buy their respect later, if you want – which is easier than you think.

Chapter 8: When/How to move on

You've heard me mention divorce already. The idea no doubt feels strange to many but the fact is that one of the best ways to secure your wealth is to get a divorce – it's just one of the quirks to how the people who rule us have decided to structure society. Everything was once unfairly balanced towards men, but some noble feminist probably died just so you could take advantage of something that has gone in favor of the fairer sex. So, you'd be dishonoring their memory and efforts if you do not. As long as you have played your cards right, you don't have to worry about a prenup. So moving onto a richer fish is the best way to go from BMW-rich to private-jet-rich in no time at all. To make this happen, you have to know when and how to throw your current catch back into their sad lonely world of being a rich bachelor, who is now 50% less rich thanks to you – who is probably something like 100,000% more rich.

Timing is the most important element here, however. You will require an air of authenticity, so you want to time your divorce for right after your current husband makes a mistake. If your divorce comes from out of the blue, then you are basically tattooing "Gold Digger" on your forehead, and will quickly go out of business. We have already explored how to divorce a dirty politician; which is perhaps the most dramatic example, but essentially the same principles apply – and all men make mistakes. If he's a complete choir boy in the bedroom then maybe he has some passionate fixation with a particular form of spirituality, which can be made to feel whacky and devilish just by pulling the right face.

Most of these rich husbands will score completely obvious own goals however. One easy way to know that you'll have an opportunity to move on is if you marry an entertainer; affairs and drunken ramblings haunt their careers like Google Images might haunt yours if you're not careful. As for athletes, they are known for having an increased level of aggression. So, one heated night of arguing and you can claim that you were fearful for your life, so you have to put your safety first and leave. Musicians are always away on tour. It'll be a matter of seconds before they will land them in bed with a sexy backup singer or event promoter. Other gold diggers will disregard that your husband or wife is already married and, without you there 24/7 to hold the reins, an affair is only a matter of time. Additionally, sometimes even gold diggers help gold diggers and occasionally, like when you see two cats suffering each others' presence and can't figure out why, this lifestyle does bring a sort of tactical unity, making for a fantastic sorority to be a part of. When your mate is away, you know other gold diggers are out there so just wait out the storm and they will make a mistake that will be grounds for divorce. Where exactly are men's brains after all.

If you married a moderately rich person the first time around and you were able to successfully pull off an "honest" divorce, now you can move up the ladder. You have a large supply of wealth that you can use to reinvest into a smaller, tighter, sexier wardrobe, a new hobby or skill, and an even better nose. Everyone and everything is supposed to receive upgrades these days. Now you're ready to go after that rich guy or gal who is going to get you your first private jet. Maybe you'll get lucky and marry your plastic surgeon. The sky is the limit once you have successfully reaped the benefits of your first divorce. Trust me, you'll never feel more love for your first mate than you do the moment you both sign those divorce papers.

Children will need to come into the picture in order to reach your maximum potential. If you go through a divorce with children and make sure that the children like you better than your mate, then you can plan to walk away with most of his or her fortune. You will be able to keep the house and the cars and make it sure that they will have to sell any collections that they have in order to afford the alimony and child support that your new lifestyle requires. Play your cards right and your monthly payments will be equal to the average person's annual salary. Allow your lawyer to argue that you were too busy to get a job because you were too busy taking care of the kids and supporting your mate. This, of course, is a lie, but the lawyer will make it work. They always do and without caring. Due to this schedule, you don't have an honest way to maintain your current lifestyle without your spouse. Now, please don't worry about the burden of having to raise the children. The fact is, your kids don't want to be with you either so you only need to be seen in public with them once or twice a month. This is a win-win for both parties. Continue to practice your basic disciplines, however, as you also need to make sure to fix any physical effects of parenthood before you decide to start working on the divorce and a new rich person to mount. You don't want to enter into a new relationship with a mom pouch or gray hair.

Children may make it tricky when you move onto a richer breed, however. It's possible that a very rich doctor or actor won't want the burden of stepchildren. You can attempt to sell the children on EBay, but this tends to break the terms of service agreement. It also may be hard to have a bikini body post baby or the time necessary to build a new gold digging relationship. So if you have plans to move up the ladder then you need to consider children carefully. They are a pain, but they can be so worth it. Especially if you succeed in molding the daughter into a mini-version of you as, when she's 21, she'll keep you in your old age. Don't get me wrong; people are living healthier and hotter for longer these days if they take care of themselves – especially rich people. Indeed, there are gold diggers staying active up to traditional retirement ages. Honestly, just take a look at the celebrity mags; you'll spot them easily and they look the part as well. It's a profession that continues to reap rewards if done properly and, because of the wonderful lifestyle you will gain, there's no wonder it becomes completely addictive.

Speaking of age, if you go down the sugar daddy route and are able to land a really big fish which is also old, this will be great for your gold digging career. The older the better. As it won't be long that they will meet the same fate as those relatives that left you their inheritance. If they have children from a previous relationship, they may be angry that you inherit their father or mother's entire wealth. But as a gold digger, that's a minor hiccup and those evil stares will be so worth it. Besides, it's for the law to take care of that, so everything will be above board. In reality, this is everything you could hope for. There's very little work involved in pleasing someone who is old, and you only have to deal with it for a short period of time. Face it, with the tight clothing you wear they'll always be one moment away from cardiac arrest. Once they die, you are free to spend their wealth to your heart's content.

On the other hand, you might not wish, or be able to carry on into your sixties. So be sure to get divorced twice before you're in your forties and, even if that luxury yacht is important to you, make sure you have sound savings and investment plans with your winnings to ensure you never need to worry about money – or falling behind the competition – ever again.

Chapter 9: Conclusion/Summary

As you can see, choosing to become a gold digger can be a very rewarding lifestyle choice. You will turn into a well versed individual who is understanding of the needs and desires within the rich community, and the people that they surround themselves with. You'll blossom into someone that lower class citizens envy and you'll acquire influential powers that will make you a force to be reckoned with among the upper class. You'll develop the ability to wear many different faces, acquire any number of skills, and create the life that everyone dreams of. You get all of these skills without ever having to worry about having a conscience. Choosing to become a gold digger may just be the best career decision that you can make.

With a bit of investment in the beginning, you can live a life where you don't have to waste a second behind a desk or in a cubicle. Who wants to spend their days putting up with people with no personality, who chew their food way too loud and smell like they work in a fried food restaurant? As a gold digger, you never have to worry about sacrificing time for money while surrounding yourself with filthy and annoying lower class citizens. Stress can be very harmful for one's health and people who work a 40–50 hour week are destined to die young and be miserable. Just look at the rest of your family as a great source for motivation when considering the alternative – which is something like whether or not to buy that blue or yellow jet ski.

You'll have a lot of sacrifices along the way. You'll need to rid your life of old friends or burdensome family members, unless they are lucky enough to die first. You can't risk them showing up in your life when you are trying to come across as impressive. If you need new friends you can buy them with the wealth that you marry into. Those people who are as shallow as you turn out to be the best friends you could hope for. They'll rarely bother you and ask you for favors because they hate you as much as you hate them. As for old friends who you really love? Well, there may be a risk-free opportunity to bring them back on board later down the line. This is not so heartless but is, in fact, the way of the world. Life does force all best friends to go separate ways whether they wish to or not, but it doesn't allow normal people to reconnect with cocktail parties and luxury cruises as you might be able to if you feel so lavish toward them someday. Although, by then you'll be such a dab hand at this that I suspect you can convince some eager suitor to pay for that too. Even if you're not going to go through it all again with this latest fling.

Whichever path you choose, make sure that you are a butterfly. You've spent your entire life as a caterpillar, munching away on the lower blades of grass while wandering through the dirt. During your transformation, hide away in a chrysalis of plastic surgery, working out, and new clothes and friends, until you are ready to emerge as a beautiful fluttering butterfly that rich people dream about catching. This is a Clark Kent/Superman type transformation, as making the decision to become a gold digger will leave you walking among royalty in the best designer clothes, at the highest class events.

Know your competition and kill it before it takes flight. Work harder than them, look better than them, and systematically destroy them. Be better than them in every element of the game. Wear a better face, fake a better life, have better clothes, have a more interesting skill. Fight hard to be the best contender in the game. For those who you can't beat, learn why that is and move on stronger.

Do your research and find out where your target breed of rich people tend to hang out. You want to plan your encounters in a way that encourages them to make the first move and creates the illusion that fate and true love are what brought your lives together. Cross paths with them at the grocery store or at the gym. Then create a situation that gives them an easy way to talk to you. Make sure you don't get stuck in a situation where you are asked to sign a prenuptial agreement. That's a gold digger's worst nightmare. It means you have failed at creating the illusion of love. Give up and go home. You can't recover from the prenup curse.

Don't hold back when you are working hard to get what you need. You will need to use some manipulation skills and step on a few toes, but it will be worth it in the end. You're a gold digger; a master of manipulation. You're a magician who pulls money out of your hats instead of rabbits. You are no worse than everyone's favorite car salesman or real estate agent, except for the fact that you're worse than them in every imaginable way. However, you know what people want, you know what makes them tick, and you use that to your advantage. Once you let go of how other people feel then you can be free to reach gold digging depths that even Anna-Nicole Smith couldn't.

Knowing when to move on from a relationship or when to retire from the life of gold digging entirely may be the trickiest part of this lifestyle choice. If you wait too long to move on from a relationship, then you may not be able to move up as far as you had hoped. If you wait too long to leave the game entirely, then you may be stuck in a marriage that has to be based around love and mutual respect and all those things that make marriage terrible.

Now you have the tools and knowledge that you need to be a successful gold digger, take a good look at yourself and move on feeling determined, optimistic and ruthless as to what lies ahead. Somewhere out there is a conquest that will see your bank account swell without any kind of working contract or terms and conditions whatsoever.

Thank you for reading my book.
I would love it if you could leave me an honest review on what you thought of this book.

If you like to know more about my books and the opportunity to be notified of free promotions please visit Aryla Publishing website

Or follow us on Facebook

Thank you

Upcoming Publications

Coming Soon Previews

How to Get a Rich Woman –
By Tyler Moses (Comedy)

Are you a man who is ready to find yourself a sugar momma? Are you tired of conforming to traditional "bread-winner" expectations? Does your 9-5 factory job take too much time away from working towards your dream of becoming a Cross-fit champion, or professional video game reviewer? As society continues to progress, it is becoming even more clear that women should be the ones to bring home the bacon. Whether an unfortunate death left her with millions or she clawed her way up to the peak of Mt. Richmore, landing yourself a wealthy woman is the best way for you to reach your goals.

It is no secret that women love power. Allowing yourself to be the beta, giving her all of the alpha power, means that everyone gets what they want. She wants to be in charge and the one who successfully conquers all traditional male roles of power and influence. You get to reap the benefits of her success. Win-win. You could not ask for a more mutually beneficial relationship.

Out Now

Sisters Book 1 – By Paula Parsons (Drama)

Your day will come. The light will eventually shine through the cracks of life. You will succeed. You will be happy. ..

Happiness...feeling whole, feeling purposeful...such a beautiful, uplifting thought.

Unfortunately, this is not my story...not even close. I wish I could tell you lies, and say that I come out in the end of all of this, feeling empowered, free, satisfied; happy...

But I don't. Not by a longshot.

My name is Melanie Loomis. I am twenty-seven years old. This is my story.........

Due for Release 2017

Julia's Story – By Lyndsey Carter (Romantic Comedy)

Julia sighed as she stepped onto the escalator. As it moved and took her up, she sighed again. Another boring day and another crammed ride home on a smelly train with no seats. She longed for some excitement, something to shake things up. She was sick of the same old, same old.

Julia boarded the train, already knowing as she craned her neck to scan each corner that there would not be any seats open. Instead, she settled for a hand-hold on the pole near the back wall. But her surroundings ceased to bother her as she stared off into the distance and let her thoughts roam. She looked at the houses she passed and imagined what type of people lived there. The train line ran at the back of the houses giving Julia a view of the garden. Some gardens had washing hanging up; others had kids' toys. Some gardens were overgrown like a mini jungle. It was a little daydream game Julie liked to play when she didn't have a book or paper to read. Soon the passing gardens and motion of the train made her eyes heavy.

Due for Release 2017

How to be a World Leader – By Tyler Moses (Comedy)

The year is 2017 and while none of us know what the future will hold at present we are at the mercy of a world leader in the USA that did not seem possible. But it has happened some ask how? Some ask why? But there is support out there so I say if he can do it then so can I and so can you!

If you are not automatically born into it and lucky enough to be an heir to a kingdom (we will also cover how to bump yourself up the ranks) if you have the unfortunate sibling line to contend with that does not put you in prime position.

In the world, we live in today with technology at our fingertips we have more control and access to information so make use of it the world is your oyster if you have visions of being the most powerful person in the world and have an unstoppable ego then this could be the job for you.

Due for Release August 2017

Visit <u>Aryla Publishing</u> website to sign up for new release books and free promotions

Printed in Great Britain
by Amazon